Chronicle of Drifting

Also by Yuki Tanaka

Poetry

Séance in Daylight (chapbook)

Translation

A Kiss for the Absolute: Selected Poems of Shuzo Takiguchi
(with Mary Jo Bang)

CHRONICLE
OF DRIFTING

YUKI TANAKA

Copper Canyon Press
Port Townsend, Washington

Cover art: Seiji Togo, *Surrealistic Stroll,* 1929. Oil on canvas, 64.0 × 48.24 cm. Sompo Museum of Art, Tokyo. © Sompo Museum of Art, 24020.

Copper Canyon Press is in residence at Fort Worden State Park in Port Townsend, Washington, under the auspices of Centrum. Centrum is a gathering place for artists and creative thinkers from around the world, students of all ages and backgrounds, and audiences seeking extraordinary cultural enrichment.

LIBRARY OF CONGRESS CATALOGING-IN-PUBLICATION DATA
Names: Tanaka, Yuki, author.
Title: Chronicle of drifting / Yuki Tanaka.
Other titles: Chronicle of drifting (Compilation)
Description: Port Townsend, Washington : Copper Canyon Press, 2025. | Summary: "A collection of poems by Yuki Tanaka"— Provided by publisher.
Identifiers: LCCN 2024048074 (print) | LCCN 2024048075 (ebook) | ISBN 9781556597053 (paperback) | ISBN 9781619323131 (epub)
Subjects: LCGFT: Poetry.
Classification: LCC PR9515.9.T36 C47 2025 (print) | LCC PR9515.9.T36 (ebook) | DDC 808.81—dc23/eng/20241230
LC record available at https://lccn.loc.gov/2024048074
LC ebook record available at https://lccn.loc.gov/2024048075

COPPER CANYON PRESS
Post Office Box 271
Port Townsend, Washington 98368
www.coppercanyonpress.org

Contents

Chronicle of Drifting

ONE

What should I compare this world to

SAMI MANSEI (EIGHTH CENTURY)

PROGNOSIS AT MIDNIGHT

I listen to the moon but it doesn't say much about my life.
Quiet night is for my cockatoo. He keeps chattering
until my neighbor comes over to complain. Then I read
a local newspaper: no murder, no robbery, one grandmother
fell down the stairs and broke her hip. I lick my inky fingers
and order my imaginary chauffeur to get ready—I'll visit her
and comfort her. I'd say, I read about you, I'm terribly sorry,
this is my cockatoo, he's twelve and loves carrots.
We'd share her hospital dinner and be happy.
Other sick people gather around us, admiring my cockatoo,
who looks proud in his cage, unfurling his light-pink wings
like stage curtains, and I'm his assistant. Grandma,
worried that I've become silent, tells me how tired I look.
"I had a series of nightmares," I say, "my boss returned
from the grave and fired me, bats attacked me like slow bullets
but bigger, I was bleeding." She says: "When I'm alone,
I paint eyes on a pear and whisper, I'm watching over you.
That makes me stronger." Back home, my body thin and healthy,
cooling my feet on a crystal ball like a psychic out of business,
I look out the window: I don't know which leaves will fall first or why.
There aren't many trees left. Not much is left of this little town.

THE VILLAGE OF THE MERMAIDS

My cat said, "Your thick green robe tastes of salt,"
and licked a satin curtain.
I have learned to sit still on a chair

in front of my house and remember our home,
where I wore a necklace of sea-foam
some called a lovely snare.

We like it here because there is less dying
under the sun: A bag of skin casts a pattern
of blue veins on the dry street. In January,

we hear voices from the distant mountains
streaked with birches and frozen pools,
and we play with our shadows. Some of us

have followed a man with a bowler hat.
He tipped it to us like a magician and said,
"There is a spell in every seashell."

He showed us how to dye a jellyfish in a bowl
of poppies, how to fatten up cocoons
with acid rain, said they taste different, do they not,

melting wriggling lives. Perfumed doorsteps,
marmalade in a glass hive, a sunlit bed
like a saffron-filled coffin—come back to this

jubilance. Think of us. Think of us engulfed
in tears—for a brother killed in war, or whatnot.

THE AIR IS AN EXQUISITE BONELESS PRINCESS

She waited for someone who wasn't like me.
If I stopped by her house, she'd stare
at the curtain's movement and dream of an ocean.

But no one else came. I tried to make her laugh
by hanging from the eaves, and she pushed me
back and forth like a swing

until my arms got tired. If I were a man
who could skip stones far enough, they'd reach
the other side of a lake, where she'd be standing.

I wore a bulky jacket to look bigger.
Once I built a ladder for her. When she started climbing,
it buckled and she fell, knocking me over.

She said, "I am the lightning, you are the tree,"
and put me back on my feet. She told me a story
she'd heard from her mariner lover about a lotus land:

"Sea spray covers your skin with salt and makes you glitter.
There you eat red flowers and forget everything.
You turn into mist, wetting robins' feathers, unnoticed,

like a shy octopus." I liked that. On a stormy day,
I wore a loose shirt and let the wind pump up my chest.
I laughed, making the air move.

DEATH IN PARENTHESES

He came home with his right leg made a bit shorter,
but they didn't notice. A landmine did it, he said
to himself, and I was the only one who heard him
because I followed him everywhere like a son.
He hobbled when no one was looking,
and I hobbled behind him.
When he plucked an iris, I plucked the one next to it,
and we thought of purple evening clouds.
When he killed a butterfly, he'd take off the wings first,
then crush it with his fingers and smell it.
I tried to catch one, but it flitted away.
He wanted to build a huge power plant
to keep us from disappearing. I nodded
and pointed out all the recent deaths, how quick they were,
tomatoes not as plump as they used to be,
the maple trees discolored, their branches
like veins with no fat around them.
All this, he decided, meant we needed new things.
But I disagreed on this: why new, why not
old me, I who have lived here for many years
even before he was born, but he didn't listen.
Mosquitoes come and go,
full and happy. Outside the window, the plant
looms over the village. It looks prettier than I thought,
which makes me want to kiss it, but I know it will
burn my lips and I won't be able to speak to anyone
with my charred mouth. I saw him
dressed up for a meeting, and they shouted,
blaming him for his empty head,
for wanting too much. The next time I saw him
he was in bed, old and delirious.

He opened his eyes, and held my hand
for the first time, and said, Don't push yourself, come back
alive. He was buried in his ever-vanishing land,
and I flew off into my friendless life.

SEASONAL PLEASURE IN THE TIME OF WAR

Tighten your cold hands around our thighs.
Eyes of raisins, charcoal nose.

Come, winter of broad shoulders.
A gift of shale is already breaking.

Sugared peels to scrub the dead skin.
Though we were injured, we would say no.

Were we here or there—we would say no.
A caterpillar stiffens on the pane.

Winter will remove our lobes.
Street light helps us read: a boy with a satchel

sailing to an island, ghosts thrown off
in a bouquet. The ship will come back

and take us away. There's plenty
of water left, our fruit well preserved.

The floor is spotted like a hard freckled back
bearing animal after animal.

A door clicks shut and we're invisible.

HOMECOMING

In the heart of a forest, a boy leans on
a light-lashed horse. He's not crying.
The horse unhurt, just as a husk
is unhurt. Lost in the forest, stroking

the frosted skin of its muscular neck,
he looks far ahead. Someone waiting.
He thinks, Make our journey last
a little longer. Say: it was a small

beautiful town. He was loved by friends.
No, he says, he had only the horse. Horse
made of white threads. Pull them out,
and the horse would lose its strength

and collapse into a man. The idea
is comforting. He could tell the horse,
who is now a man, he is tired
and cannot go on.

I WAS BORN IN A MOUNTAIN NEXT TO MY BROTHER

1

Wolf skins kept us warm.
The cave yawned and swallowed
our cries for food. Our aunt came
to rescue us. Afraid for us
when we didn't sweat,
she gathered rain in a pail
and washed our bodies.

We had dimples and used them
to our benefit: She fed us milk,
bird, dog in a basket woven
like fingers praying for something.
Then it hailed. She said
that's a monster scuttling on the roof,
looking for you, so keep quiet.
We did, only to burst out laughing
when she left. There was a time

when a spiderweb was our shirt,
the moon a butterfly caught
in our retina. Now we are old
enough to be useful. While we work
a pinecone falls and cuts my skin.

Blood, isn't it, my brother says,
and licks. Once, troubled by night,
we crawled through the mud
until our knees hit a buried wheel.
We thought it was the stairs
to a hidden room where our family
would be waiting with a bloodline.

2

A man drowned in a river.
We scoop up the water
and look at his face. Inside
his egg-shaped head, a white
spasm—death looks like birth.

We chew a fat magnolia
and trudge forward, following
drumbeats from distant lanterns.
My brother is as thin as a wet doll.
I stroke his back as a mother would.

A birch sways like a stream
of sand, making us long for rain.
When we arrive at a village,
we see from behind the bush
a bonfire, men and women
dancing around it, a ruddy
sweaty circle, calling spirits
home. They all look well fed.
They all look happy.

To join them, we must learn
their moves, the way
they submit to the rhythm.
We raise our arms
and step toward the light,
pushed by soft hands with the force
that rips the stem from petals.
We find ourselves in the center.

3

They try to fatten us. I work
as a salt maker, burning seaweed.
My brother sleeps on the barley mat.
The doctor says nothing is wrong
with his lungs, but his stomach
is very bad. He's getting thinner.

He's a cicada shell that lets in
too much light. What is his next body?
A blue azalea, a gull falling—
I might not recognize him once he's gone.
His eyes reflect my face. His breath,
thick as a moth, brushes my cheek.

At night I eat alone. When he wakes up,
he says he dreamed of our parents
in a warm house, and he was a butterfly
clinging to their window. When I hold
a bowl to his mouth, he shakes his head.

Pale face, pale fingers, salmon-red lips
trapped in moonlight. He's the more
beautiful of the two, and kinder.
The smoke of myrrh circles his pupils.
He's tired. He's dying into another life.

LIKE ONE WHO HAS MINGLED FREELY WITH THE WORLD

I cannot fly. I jump and jump to imitate a bird.
Surrounded by children, I leap up
with a huge silk scarf around my shoulders

to look like a crane. They laugh and laugh
and push me into a rabbit skin and watch.
At night I glint with long ears and peep through

a window misted with the steam from a teakettle,
hoping that they'll let me in. I'm mostly alone.
They want to keep me as a legend:

invisible, silly, a hopeless woman-chaser.
That's what I was to the girl in a wedding kimono.
She screamed when I popped up from the rice paddy

like a big frog. There's no harm in me except some
occasional cuts. They're meant to remind you of life.
Dirty, honest, lonely—if the sun was a pool

of red ink, I'd dive in and come out
beautiful, tanned, cancerous. Death
might cheer me up, make me feel

more human. Perched on a wooden fence,
I hold an umbrella up against the clear sky,
but no bird or animal falls from the sun.

It looks bigger than yesterday, like a bad sore
some geese have pecked at over and over, and now
it's bulging, festering, ready to gush down

and drown us. I won't tell anyone about it. I wait.
It might drop some riches, some food, some wings.

TWO

In 1904, thirteen "geisha girls" visited the
St. Louis World's Fair, to be exhibited.

EXHIBITION OF DESIRE

Would you like a slice of pear or a slice
of amethyst? Both taste of nightmare, and we,

mice in silk kimonos, rustle across
a fragile bridge. Nearly identical, sick

of the vast, Midwestern sky, quiet as dry
starfish. Eyed, dipped in a basin, a beautiful

bundle of nerves. I remember
a harvest behind the curtain, that white

swollenness in the Spring Room: a throat
frosted to the bone, and then

the tremor of gelatin beneath the skin—
grass in the mouth, green breath in winter.

I was hidden in hydrangeas, free of melanin,
waiting for a gush of blue feathers

from the stalk of a jaded sunflower.
Then, the endless curiosity

of earth: a muddy river in the distance
saturated me as the soul lingers in the body

to feel its sinews unravel, raw—
my little island at war. A brazier warms

a windowful of eyes. There are no flowers like us,
patient or numbed. There is no hunger

like ours, seducers of scattered beauty.
Emptied of blazing organs, we flew lightly,

then pulled, sunk beneath, by wanting.

THE EMPIRE OF LIGHT

We are asked to stand at the pond. A sudden light
drowns us. Four empty turtles filled with flowers.

We use our bodies to grasp a foreign tongue.
Red-eyed fingers, porcelain skin, dark eyelashes

that never fall. Come, we say in unison, and they come
as ants gather around a slowly loosening sugar cube.

Here is a bowl to keep us whole. Here is a peacock fan
to cool our foreheads. On a rainy day,

we furnish our room with pink shells, pink imitation lips.
There is no ocean here. A stuffed bird on the mantel

has a calm look. Hunted in sleep, gutted,
the senses all dried up—thirst, terror. A fake crane

in the garden waits for spring. Droplets on the window
swarm over marigolds like blind bees.

The tip of my long hair can disturb the water
as squid ink overflows a delicate vial.

Soon I am going home. Changed, forgotten—
a girl in a barren field, pressing twilight to her throat.

THE BODY IN FRAGMENTS

She drinks peppermint tea for the first time.

It cools her as if winter hurried just for her.

Outside, humid air ballooning a shirt on a clothesline.

At night the mist becomes so thick it feels like a person.

Once she placed a green bottle on the porch to gather him

and drink dregs of him, her teeth hidden.

Daily practice of English: *maze, meteor, marsh.*

Advanced level: *marzipan, mating, mesmerized.*

In return, she teaches Japanese. *Mizu* is water,

matsu to wait, homonym for pine tree (chuckle of confusion).

Mizu o matsu, to long for water.

If she were an ocean, she would overflow.

She loves *marsh*—the ooze, the thickness of it.

She opens her mouth wide enough to swallow a small tangerine

but the word comes out wrong, overripe,

making her jaw ache. Her flaw charms her guests

like a glass eye in a comely face.

The Japanese *numa,* she says, represents the wary gait of a farmer,

nu one step, *ma* next, so as not to sink.

You could eat wind and be thin and afloat,

or you have to be the weight of an eyelash.

I marsh you. She means to hold her lover in her arms

and allow him to sink—earth at its tenderest, most welcoming—

until he is clean flesh.

Persimmon is *kaki,* every labial sliced off, angular.

We have no persimmon, they say, so try this for your tea ceremony,

and they give her a slice of pear, dotted with an evening gnat.

She scratches the gnat off with the tine of a fork,

and blows it onto her palm.

She wishes she could blow a mole off her chin like that,

the size of a sesame seed, the only defect on her snowy skin.

But with whose breath—lover, mother,

or one of the girls who seem clean.

I'd ask her to eat this pear first and sweeten her breath.

When she blows on my chin, I will close my eyes and become

a swaying field of wheat.

A gift arrives—gossamer from Virginia, wrapped in tissue paper.

At dawn it falls over her shoulder.

She takes it off at noon and folds it over her lap,

now heavier, having absorbed her sweat,

and finally hers.

A mirror makes her worried about a gap between her front teeth.

Soon, abundant winter hair,

a sick planetarium spinning in her skull.

Sora is the sky, *kumo* the clouds, which also means spider.

A spider eats clouds to make a web

in which she is caught with her parents and her lover.

When she moves, the web trembles and they look for her.

Ue means both hunger and above, so she looks up

when she is hungry. A cloud breaks into mouthfuls

and fills her. At dinner, they give her a glass rabbit,

one foot missing. She presses him against

her powdered neck, hoping he will mistake it

for a snowy hill. When she looks out the window

for a new landscape, she thinks, If I carry that meadow

folded in my pocket and spread it back home,

our cows will go mad. In the middle of the meadow,

a night lake with a pleasure boat. She wants

to touch its soft pupil, make it blink and swallow her.

THREE

I thought I was the only one drifting
on a night boat

Unknown

If only the sky were kind enough to lend me his blue coat. I bought a piece of tuna at the fish market. The owner's apron was so clean he must have one for greeting, one for gutting. The fringe of his right thumbnail a red crescent. I gave him two 500-yen coins beaded with my sweat, and he wiped them on his chest. Summer is coming to a close—autumn ahead, trailing orange hair. Walking down the alley lined with small buddha statues, I was reminded of a friend who would pray at night. She knelt and prayed to a picture of her altar on her laptop so hard she cried for the health of her parents. I thought, Dark-haired cloud with beautiful rain.

Surgery on Monday. No eating the night before, no liquid, no thought of liquid, just empty your head like a brand-new flower vase. Moving to Tokyo has changed my mindset—never stop, never wait. In the mountains, I could stand in the rain, like a parsnip waiting to be pulled up by the hair. Sometimes I stand on the street corner and watch: It is difficult to locate a lover in a crowd. When they say there's a storm coming, I prepare by imagining a sturdy brick house. When they say there'll be an earthquake, I wish for shoes.

I feel nothing and go to a café to be seen. Cappuccino rings inside my paper cup look like a Baumkuchen universe. A white man in line, with black-rimmed glasses, gawks at me, and utters the word *creepy,* thinking I wouldn't understand. If my toes were sharper, I would kick his Achilles' heel. How can one listen to oneself thinking ill of others. You can look into the mean man's head and find cosmos like mine, perhaps more beautiful. I stopped by a shrine to wash my hands, but it was too cold. When I am not walking, I liquefy. I want to be a stagnant pool of water reflecting a face.

A long faculty meeting about punctuation, the aesthetics of powerpoint. At school, I feel minuscule. Teach English class until 3 and go to a museum and see a live hermit crab, which migrates from shell to shell, and for whom the artist has made a glass castle to live in. I can't invite anyone into my head because it is not comfortable. From the fifth floor, I watch a policeman at a zebra crossing ushering pedestrians. He whistles, moving his arms, clutching a red baton. I wish I could tell him he sounds like a sea kite, but would he be offended. I want to simplify my life. Look up, I say, and he looks up.

A doctor with horn-rimmed glasses was kind, despite the horn. A ginkgo leaf, attached to a spider's thread, pirouettes on my way home, celebrating my getting better. My toes wiggle, pupa-like—I hope they won't leave me. My face—a map with broken rivers. Caught in an evening shower, I swing my hair to imitate a wet willow. I'd love to be pushed and walk and walk faster. Loveless, I buy a hard persimmon at the grocery store, hoping it will soften overnight when I'm imagining sweetness.

I'm reading a book about thirteen geisha who boarded a steamer to America to attend the 1904 World's Fair in St. Louis, as part of the Japanese exhibit. One of them wore a blue kimono, carried a purse that contained a bar of soap, a muslin cloth, an incense bag full of chrysanthemum seeds, a reminder of her home. On the third day, she found a dead mackerel on the deck. She planted a seed in the gill of the fish and put it in a ceramic vase. A week later, a bud grew out of its mouth, the green stalk had reached its tail, overwhelming the rot with tender fragrance. They called her *the girl who skewered the fish with a flower.*

Two words for "heart." *Kokoro* means heart in a moral, spiritual sense; it never refers to the organ. *Shinzo,* it always does. I prefer *kokoro*—the round vowels lightly knock at my heart like a shy guest afraid to startle the host. Ginkgo trees are thriving in Tokyo. Ginkgo is *icho,* a homonym of 胃腸, "stomach and guts." Instead of turning yellow, *icho* stays red and livid. In my mind, the heart is tired and wants to rest.

A stray cat in an alley in Yotsuya. I had no food but I made a gesture of food inviting the cat but she didn't come. The locksmith there was wonderful, taught me how to fix my apartment key, which had been bent when it got too close to a kerosene stove at the train station. He reheated it with a burner, until the key glowed in front of us, and he used pliers to unbend it, like setting a broken tail straight. The cat in my head cried in pain, but I patted her to be quiet. Went home with a bag of strawberries, lettuce, oysters, but my head was full of dry things. Someone walking outside. Voice of a sweet-potato seller with a shy trumpet. I can't make music, not being a piano. But as a child, I kicked sand into the ferns, making the sound of light rain.

How lovely was the horse walking into our alley. The smell of soy sauce from a former distillery made the pure white horse more human. A can of candy from grandfather's haversack hidden in the closet—I was going to feed the horse, but grandmother unclenched the can from me, though the candy was already in my mouth. Taste of dull sugar, as the horse walked past our house, led by grandmother's friend who was an herb doctor. I asked for peppermint to cleanse my mouth, moved my tongue across the back of my lower teeth as I watched the huge teeth of the horse, brownish, they said, from eating too many apples. Clack clack. I wished I could clack clack to wake my family up at night, to be noticed. Clack clack to wish the storm away. Grandmother stroked the mane of the horse, but I wasn't small enough to be lifted up and touch him. How I wanted to go to the beach and stroke the white sand while thinking of that horse.

During the *bon* festival, I spotted a glazed apple on the stone pavement. Ghosts in purple kimonos circled us as mother rubbed my cheek with a hemp handkerchief. The cloth against my cheek sounded like a boy walking through the snow. I said, Thud thud, but she asked me to stop because my breath tickled her ear. At a noodle stand, we bought a bowl of udon with chopped green onions, and I ate it while watching a boy crouch at a long low table, holding a needle, carving out a figure from a sugar plate the size of a postage stamp—the figure of a dog because it was the Year of the Dog. When the sugar dog broke in half, we kept walking. A fluff of cotton candy drifted by, and I followed it, trying to lick the air.

The funeral of an uncle who had studied in England. On New Year's Eve, he'd open our door, come straight to me, and squeeze my cheeks with his hands, saying, Here's my brazier. In his coffin I placed a box of red macaroons, but one of them was covered with ants. Mother said, He'd eat it, thinking it was covered with sesame seeds. Before his funeral, I made a snowman and buried a persimmon in its trunk. After the funeral, I pulled it out and ate it. The snowman had no legs—otherwise, he'd leave us, move to a colder place, and our population would thin out. Wanting softness, I leaned on the snow and let my body freeze, my eyes growing cold as winter eggs.

My fingers are so delicate they seem to belong to a better hand, but not having that ideal hand, they came to me. Yellow icicles, dripping after a dish wash. Quiet night is ahead, but I'm not ready. I sit on my chair wishing to be a seagull skimming the ocean so by the time I've come to your shore, salt has formed on my belly and you can scrape it.

A trip to Kyoto. I wear a mask and read *Snow Country* on the train, feeling disinfected and happy. The alert is set off and the train stops in the middle of a rice field. The jingling of my apartment keys in my pocket seems to say this is our home, where is the door. A man sitting opposite me takes a banana from his briefcase and peels and eats and keeps on reading. Outside, a sun-freckled farmer glances at us, then keeps watch over a bonfire where he must be burning leaves to fertilize the land. The man opposite me is mesmerized by the farmer. When he wipes the window with his finger, the field enters his forehead, leaving in him a flame. I stay empty, a blue outline.

A gray high-rise at night, all windows lit, except two—they huddle, like a pair of dreaming panthers. Christmas song in the air. A top-hatted boy hums the tune while handing out pocket tissues. I say no thanks but Merry Christmas (his breath is white, feathery). The cold air is chiseling me into a better person. A month ago, I cut my fingertip, sliced off a piece of skin, small as a grain of rice, and it has grown back, which makes me happy. I buy a meat bun on a street corner. When I break it in half, I turn around to see the bun seller, but he is already out of reach. In another life, we could be mist together, bodiless, feelingless, making our city glisten. A glass bakery with no one in it. Laughter of someone I will never meet. I walk along the river, thinking I too can flow, mirroring the bluebells.

The first haircut in six months. Inside the salon, the scent of citron colors my sight into gentle orange as my hair is scissored. If I were a pine, there'd be green hair around me, and a scent of pine. My deer-eyed hairdresser says she's leaving Tokyo and starting her own salon in her hometown. She complains about the pace of the city, and I agree—sad momentum. Outside, the sound of a church bell, which cleans the air inside, glass-like. It seems everyone is going home. Before she goes, I want her to look into my head like a crystal ball. I'd say, "There is a boat and we are in it." We'd linger a little, drink sake and compose poetry. "Here," I'd say, "is a cup of evening light. Articulate your feeling at sunset."

I eat hot pot with my novelist friend in Shibuya. She is writing a story about a man who knocks on a door and introduces himself as a block of cheese, but since there are no mice, he is not let in. We haven't seen each other for a year, which means we might or might not meet next year, but we are here. After dinner, we go to an underground bar. The bartender smells of lemon, as if she played hide-and-seek in a lemon grove and just came out. When we part at the train station, we promise to do this again, maybe in America. On my way home, I ask the sky to come down and keep me company, but the sky prefers its own boundlessness.

FOUR

You have departed on a long road.

SANO NO CHIGAMI NO OTOME
(EIGHTH CENTURY)

GHOST IN WAITING

He watches me through the oleander bush.
The rain has softened his cigarette—

he is burning still. A jar of plums cools underground,
maturing the flesh. He lingers inside the flames,

his hair like weeds grasping a stone, the bones
breaking, until what's left is the scraped roof

of a mouth. Afterheat resists the morning chill.
Unshriveled. We are not separate.

His scent reddens the hour. The air thickens
as the smoke enters the room. I wish for a breeze

that animates my hair—I will not suffocate a bee.
Pollen over his bright chest. What grows from where

to what. Trapped heat. Dirt. Thick gauze
on a wound that heals and unheals in sweat.

AFTERLIFE

1

my body thinned

to a mirror reflecting others back

mrs mashino stumbled and fell

and I helped her up saying you are a scarecrow

tumbled by a flood she said she was and I felt bad

I should have said, You were happy on the cloud

and fell down with heavy thoughts

how her mood shifted from rain to storm to magnolia

her small face had a pockmarked cheek

but sweat made it a beautiful riverbank

mice music from the buoys

unbraided hair her fireworks

don't feed stray cats or they'll make light of you

she had the voice of grass

and I imitate the wind passing through her

haha she laughs haha I echo

mingled with the shells of Ishikawa

2

I wait for her return

sitting in the distance of forty pebbles

slow rain from the icicles

it is windless

the horse hoofprint becomes a sunlit pool

my tree blooms and bears plums

and lets them fall

like guests knocking on earth unable to come in

does that mountain have a chin

where a bird could perch and tickle him

if the mountain speaks up

the bird is shaken off and needs to find a home

my smoothed arm is a desirable branch

come fly to touch me

are you too a reincarnator

you have that forsythia look

ANATOMY

Shallow river with my right foot in it.

The river has no fish, but a dozen sundown snakes

nibble at my toes. I feel no poison. I am strong.

My toenails hang on to me like lovers.

When I am tired, I leap up to relax the muscles or squat

to dip my buttocks in the water. My left foot dives

in the river, like a child. The bright snakes welcome him.

Under the watery roof, my feet are brother and sister.

From their viewpoint, my face is smooth as otter skin,

which gives me the confidence to say, You are both invited.

Man with a liquid face, they call me, but refuse to come out.

My face streams, carrying dirt.

The evening turns my eyes to geraniums.

I gulp to beautify my voice, and say, Come home.

They whisper, He can't get his own feet back,

is he a ghost.

Having no feet, he must miss the smell of crushed grass.

DISCOURSE ON VANISHING

1

I will start with modern inventions: growth,

abundance, which brought out a world

filled with the dying. Nothing happens.

Children, echoing brooks, hard jaws yawning

in the background. Our place knows us,

our pulsations. This fleeting desire

to last longer, shadowed by clouds

that pass away as soon as we focus

on the sky. Broken ghost. The sun is cold

but does not come to an end. Stasis, deadlock.

Animate this landscape. There is no birdsong.

2

Look at puppets performing

with consciousness. The waves dilate

without order. Glutted heart. The waves,

claiming unity, unrelieved rhythm,

progress, breaking on shore.

                              She weaves

waves and light, remembering waves and birds.

The hand hidden behind the wool. She tries

to capture a blue flower as it vanishes

in a garden. Again and again. What seems to be

its murmur endures. Clipped murmur. Deep-blue

ripple: "He is dead." "He is dead."

3

This blue already fading beneath the waves

which threaten to encrust a diver. Mist

pours into the body, formless, real

like a child. This new world at the end of pain

remains the same. The night descends

over houses. They are robbed of windows,

give out daylight. The darkness washing

the mist from the fields, grazing the eye.

Now, life can swerve, leaving the afterimage

of its absence: an old wine bottle and behind it,

the arm of a woman, green sky flickering.

4

The next landscape introduces a fire.

The fire is real. There is no speech.

When a boy collapses over the basin,

a dream comes, already posthumous:

sunken streets, valleys full of faces,

a young horse yearning for strength.

This is an end in view, beginning

over and over. People spring to life,

watching the breath of a wounded animal.

A faint chirping from somewhere—

unseen, forgotten cages.

5

Her fever is difficult. She complains

about spots. The cold laughter of a man

who suffers in a burning dress.

Waltzes playing. Uncontrollable laughter.

A Salome dances, replaced by another

in quick succession, confused.

The night falls flat in a crowded room.

A woman tries to talk, unable to turn her eyes

from a body struck outside. Bright light—

no more. The earth stays still again.

This is not the end of the broken world.

ONE ARM

A bare white arm
disinfected. Plump, sizzling.
Should I let it speak, or just imagine
it speaks? Beauty

in a dustbin.
A panda in pantaloons.
The moon paisleyed on a doily.
Delicious disfigurement.

That arm
bared for the first time in the spring—
blue perfume moistened
my mouth. A made thing.

As if I had forgotten how
hardtack stuck in the molars,
how I could not salivate for thirst.
As if I had forgotten

roofless stations, the burns.
A car's headlights skid through the mist
like hyperemic eyes.
Pigeons on the mezzanine

pulped to feathers. Laminated fairies
—made things. A letter from Mishima:
"House of the Sleeping Beauties" is unusual
for formal perfection.

Like a frozen sparrow. The arm
peppered with antiseptics. Let it
speak. The pulse
of a detached arm.

The first sentence: "I can let you have
one of my arms for the night."
She tears her arm off
and places it on my knee.

AUBADE

I sit on a chair and the chair touches me back.
According to my chair, I have two hips
and bones inside them hard as peach pits.

The femurs connected to the pelvis
lead to the kneecaps. I have kneecaps.
In the ancient past of my village, people used them

as drinking cups: a boy sipping sake
from the kneecap of grandfather,
whose kneecap is bigger than grandmother's.

She helps her son detach the kneecap from the leg
and wash it in the stream. White of the kneecap,
she thinks, is trembling like a moon.

Funny it smells sweeter than the knee of the man
she remembers. When he was alive,
he wasn't much of a man—thin, boneless,

his shoulder soft as a berry-bearing ivy.
Funny he seems more alive now,
this trembling bone under the cold water.

SÉANCE IN DAYLIGHT

She opened her mouth as if her throat were a bird
ready to leave her. I thought she was going to sing

for the dead, because she said she always saw them.
I was cold. I snuggled against her like a tall cat.

When she put the petals of a hydrangea on my eyelids,
I heard rain pattering behind them,

and I was a window from which she saw her friends
return: lights lit inside them, now alive, now burning,

moths in a struggle to escape their own wings
edged with fire. She waved at them and spoke

through me, fogging my skin with words I couldn't hear.
I wasn't cold anymore, her breath so warm, her cheek

pressed against the fragile glass, which was my body.

EVIDENCE OF NOCTURNE

Whatever is singing above, come down.
Drink a lake from my eyes, fever and azaleas

both thriving on the shore.
Don't eat when your mouth is dry—

even a scrap of bread makes you bleed.
Withdraw. No lion devours the bones

of a beloved. Tonight, after rain
I'd like you to fly through these irises,

your blue mustache, blue cheeks
infected with sky. You can be frail here.

Between the clouds, a moonlit plane,
a thousand houses to be washed away.

This pile of wood wished to be a stairway
but couldn't. Will you pretend to climb it.

Notes

The epigraphs at the beginning of sections one, three, and four are from poems found in the *Manyoshu,* the oldest extant anthology of Japanese poetry, compiled in the eighth century. All translations are mine.

"The Village of the Mermaids" was inspired by the painting of the same title by Paul Delvaux. The line "There is a spell in every seashell" is adapted from a line in H.D.'s book-length poem *The Walls Do Not Fall* (1944).

The title "The Air Is an Exquisite Boneless Princess" is taken from "Document d'Oiseaux: Documenting Birds," a poem by Shuzo Takiguchi, cotranslated by myself and Mary Jo Bang. Our translation first appeared on the *Boston Review* website for National Poetry Month 2015, and later in *A Kiss for the Absolute: Selected Poems of Shuzo Takiguchi* (Princeton University Press, The Lockert Library of Poetry in Translation Series, 2024).

"Homecoming" is based on *For the Road* (1951), a painting by Jack B. Yeats.

"Like One Who Has Mingled Freely with the World" was inspired by *Kamaitachi* (1969), a book of photographs by Japanese avant-garde photographer Eikoh Hosoe.

"Exhibition of Desire," "The Empire of Light," and "The Body in Fragments" were inspired by photographs of Japanese women who went to St. Louis to participate in the 1904 World's Fair. The poem "The Empire of Light" takes the title of a series of paintings by René Magritte.

"Chronicle of Drifting" is named after Kansuke Yamamoto's 1949 collage of the same title.

Part 1 of "Afterlife" ends with a line from a poem by Yosami no Otome, which is included in the *Manyoshu*.

"Discourse on Vanishing" is an erasure of the first half of my doctoral dissertation "Tempo and Temporality in Anglo-American Modernist Literature." The poem draws on the language of Virginia Woolf's *The Waves* and Djuna Barnes's *Nightwood*.

"One Arm" is based on the short story of the same title by Japanese novelist Yasunari Kawabata. The quotation "I can let you have one of my arms for the night" comes from Edward Seidensticker's translation.

Acknowledgments

I would like to thank the editors of the following journals in which these poems first appeared, sometimes in earlier versions:

The American Poetry Review: "The Air Is an Exquisite Boneless Princess," "Homecoming," "Like One Who Has Mingled Freely with the World"

Denver Quarterly: "One Arm"

DIAGRAM: "Discourse on Vanishing"

Gulf Coast: "Prognosis at Midnight"

The Hopkins Review: "Afterlife," "Anatomy"

The Kenyon Review: "Evidence of Nocturne," "Ghost in Waiting"

The Margins: from "Chronicle of Drifting," "Séance in Daylight," "The Village of the Mermaids"

The Nation: "The Body in Fragments"

New England Review: from "Chronicle of Drifting"

The New Republic: from "Chronicle of Drifting"

Oxford Poetry (UK): from "Chronicle of Drifting"

The Paris Review: "Aubade"

Poetry: from "Chronicle of Drifting," "Death in Parentheses"

The Poetry Review (UK): from "Chronicle of Drifting"

West Branch: "The Empire of Light," "Exhibition of Desire," "I Was Born in a Mountain next to My Brother"

"Death in Parentheses" was reprinted in *Best New Poets 2017.*

Some of these poems appeared in my chapbook *Séance in Daylight* (Bull City Press, 2018).

This book has been in the making since 2014 and could not exist without friends who have supported my writing all these years. Special thanks to Shangyang Fang, Rachel Heng, Carl Jeanbart, Veronica Martin, Suphil Lee Park, Yanbing Tan, Olga Vilkotskaya, and Emily Jungmin Yoon.

To my teachers, whose wisdom and passion have shaped how I read and write poetry: Henri Cole, Natalie Diaz, Robert von Hallberg, Paul Harding, Jane Miller, Naomi Shihab Nye, Lisa Olstein, Vivian Pollak, Roger Reeves, Vincent Sherry, and the late Dean Young.

To the faculty, staff, and my cohort at the Michener Center for Writers for creating a community where we could believe that art matters. Special thanks to Marla Akin, who took me to a hospital and kept me company there during a difficult time. I'm forever indebted to your kindness.

To the following institutions for providing financial and artistic support that enabled me to write: the Bread Loaf Writers' Conference, the Community of Writers, the Fine Arts Work Center, the Frost Place, the Juniper Summer Writing Institute, the Michener Center for Writers, and the New York State Summer Writers Institute.

To Ashley E. Wynter, Ryo Yamaguchi, and everyone at Copper Canyon Press: Thank you for believing in my work and guiding me through every stage of the publication process.

To my parents: Long after I had embarked on this artistic path, my mother told me that when she was young, she used to write poems in Japanese and recorded them in a notebook she titled "Hydrangea." I'm glad to have unknowingly carried on her mantle.

Finally, endless gratitude to Mary Jo Bang, teacher, cotranslator, and friend. She was the first person to take my ambition to write in English seriously and provided much-needed guidance. She read every single poem I wrote with her inimitable X-ray eye and helped me improve them. Most important of all, she showed me by her example what it means to live in this world as an artist. Thank you.

About the Author

Yuki Tanaka was born and raised on a small island in Yamaguchi, Japan. His poems have appeared in *The Nation, The New Republic, The Paris Review, Poetry,* and elsewhere. He has also cotranslated, with Mary Jo Bang, *A Kiss for the Absolute: Selected Poems of Shuzo Takiguchi,* published by Princeton University Press. He received an MFA from the Michener Center for Writers at the University of Texas at Austin, and a PhD in English from Washington University in St. Louis. He lives in Tokyo and teaches at Hosei University.

Poets for Poetry

Copper Canyon Press poets are at the center of all our efforts as a nonprofit publisher. Poets not only create the art that defines our books, but they read and teach the books we publish. Many are also generous donors who believe in financially supporting the larger poetry community of Copper Canyon Press. For decades, our poets have quietly donated their royalties, have directly engaged in our fundraising campaigns, and have made personal donations in support of the next generation. Their support has encouraged the innovative risk-taking that sustains and furthers the art form.

The donor-poets who have contributed to the Press since 2023 include:

Jonathan Aaron
Kelli Russell Agodon
Pamela Alexander
Joyce Harrington Bahle
Ellen Bass
Mark Bibbins
Sherwin Bitsui
Marianne Boruch
Laure-Anne Bosselaar
Cyrus Cassells
Peter Cole and Adina Hoffman
Elizabeth J. Coleman
John Freeman
Forrest Gander
Jenny George
Daniel Gerber
Julian Gewirtz
Jorie Graham
Robert and Carolyn Hedin
Bob Hicok
Ha Jin
Jaan Kaplinski
Laura Kasischke

Jennifer L. Knox
Ted Kooser
Deborah Landau
Sung-Il Lee
Ben Lerner
Dana Levin
Heather McHugh
Jane Miller
Lisa Olstein
Gregory Orr
Eric Pankey
Kevin Prufer
Paisley Rekdal
James Richardson
Alberto Ríos
David Romtvedt
Natalie Shapero
Arthur Sze
Elaine Terranova
Chase Twichell
Ocean Vuong
Connie Wanek-Dentinger
Emily Warn

Poetry is vital to language and living. Since 1972, Copper Canyon Press has published extraordinary poetry from around the world to engage the imaginations and intellects of readers, writers, booksellers, librarians, teachers, students, and donors.

WE ARE GRATEFUL FOR THE MAJOR SUPPORT PROVIDED BY:

academy of american poets

THE PAUL G. ALLEN
FAMILY FOUNDATION

Hawthornden Foundation

McSWEENEY'S

TO LEARN MORE ABOUT UNDERWRITING
COPPER CANYON PRESS TITLES,
PLEASE CALL 360-385-4925 EXT. 105

WE ARE GRATEFUL FOR THE MAJOR SUPPORT PROVIDED BY:

Anonymous

Jill Baker and Jeffrey Bishop

Anne and Geoffrey Barker

Donna Bellew

Lisha Bian

Will Blythe

John Branch

Diana Broze

John R. Cahill

Sarah J. Cavanaugh

Keith Cowan and Linda Walsh

Peter Currie

Geralyn White Dreyfous

The Evans Family

Mimi Gardner Gates

Gull Industries Inc.
    on behalf of William True

Carolyn and Robert Hedin

David and Jane Hibbard

Bruce S. Kahn

Phil Kovacevich and Eric Wechsler

Maureen Lee and Mark Busto

Ellie Mathews and Carl Youngmann
    as The North Press

Larry Mawby and Lois Bahle

Petunia Charitable Fund and
    adviser Elizabeth Hebert

Suzanne Rapp and Mark Hamilton

Adam and Lynn Rauch

Emily and Dan Raymond

Joseph C. Roberts

Cynthia Sears

Kim and Jeff Seely

Tree Swenson

Julia Sze

Barbara and Charles Wright

In honor of C.D. Wright
    from Forrest Gander

Caleb Young as C. Young Creative

The dedicated interns and faithful
    volunteers of Copper Canyon Press

The pressmark for Copper Canyon Press
suggests entrance, connection, and interaction
while holding at its center
an attentive, dynamic space for poetry.

This book is set in MVB Embarcadero Pro and Dashiell Text.
Cover design by Becca Fox Design.
Book design by Claretta Holsey.

www.ingramcontent.com/pod-product-compliance
Lightning Source LLC
Jackson TN
JSHW022241080325
80367JS00003B/7